BECAUSE I CAN

DREAM

BY RICHARD JUMAH

FOR KARA

CONTENTS

3

1. A SPIRAL OF LEAVES

a day like today

a spiral of leaves in the whisked up wind
scratches at my ears

I hear through my mind they are hands of
souls

but they are curled up and dead

returning to buds so the ground be fed

the weight of the world is turning in
autumn

the day is bold and gray

the farms and the city are closer together

like love between lovers that meet in the
end

now time passes quicker than ever

the night will arrive when the children
are fed

the tears in our eyes could sink us
forever

unless we pick up our world and put it to
bed

the levels of life are are perched upon
limbs

except for the fish that are without wings

but the day will come when the tide rises
higher

we could save the world with days like
today

beyond the stars

love is not waiting for angels to fall

or caging a bird that sings to them all

love is the power we all have inside

that flexes the heart and feels like a ride

inside that realm a secret a spell

how many we love how many we tell

of the size of our feelings and why we
cant see

that love has its borders and bridges the
sea

under the sun love is still trying

the night has begun and the moon it is
sighing

from wishes so earthly attracting its mass

we all feel that force the feeling at last

so why we go hungry not feeding the
flesh

is because love is a power not equal to
death

but love is a hunger it's size beyond stars

and who doesn't have it is headed for
mars.

blue white and gold

weeds in the world that we will want rice

which one a remedy for hearts that are
heavy

fruits of the Forrest for birds love the
berry

but which one a poison out of the many

whales in the water telling their tale

the silence the slaughter and the ships
that are gone

out of our story the business of blood

into a world where there isn't a god

birds in the sky the opposite of scales

who do they judge in the freedom of air

when witness to weather that we have
created

the desert has vultures for a world that is
dated

bees in the world that there will be honey

the choice of the flowers for queens that make more

royal is the duty guarding these towers

where our hands pick our feet do not fall

enter the evening blue white and gold

before the sunsets breaking the mold

in the green brown and black night will wake

from the gold in the mold the humans would take.

empty they float

a bowl holds much rice empty they float

the boats are in the world that people
have hope

freedom flys ahead of swords cut
through with rust

words are nearly dead instead the people
trust

their god to light their way so enemies
are lost

upon their evil ways money has a cost

should I reach into my pocket for money
to buy a gun

when what we have as money could be
killing everyone

should I preach the word to a feathered
bird

that will never see the sun

or dig the turkey Christmas that is saving every one

from the year of work it took to reap and sow the land

the page is in the book where fields will turn to sand

tomorrow is another day where war and famine scream

the words that we cant hear that life is just a dream

choose the wage of life and wake up with a soul

be a reason why there's god and why the truth is told

raise the blood into your hearts feel its beating wings

and hold your head up high because the caged bird sings.

2. IT IS NOT FEAR

ETERNAL EYE

it is not fear why I side with god

is the soul of a human inside a dog

why do frogs legs kick when dead

why say grace when dogs are fed

when I'm dead I'll kick like a horse

and bite at every single choice

because language costed me a voice

what words would grow upon a tree

that all could take away and read

the leaves have lines like in your palm

the fruit falls from it's branched arm

inside the fruit the size of seeds

that live beyond the hundred years

and in a hundred who'll be there

to pick the fruit or clean the air

the leaves do tell of it's healthy state

but for the world is it too late

house of hope

welcome to the house of hope

beyond the distance that we cope

release your fear of failing to the wind

what blows from the past to the future

know the maps have not the beauty of
the hills and valleys

and what is written in lines has only
direction

what losses we have seen are not the
answers to our people

and what our people ask for is only
freedom

hold up only such light as would light
this house

and let go of death what at best is only mercy

let your soul dance upon the world without worry

let rain make you happy where others would cry

rest only when you reach this house

and bring only what you have of love

then love will wake you from the everlasting sleep

that weighs upon the weak and weary

let no one take that waking force from you

and know that in creating the world god was also alone

this house of hope is built upon all human effort

and without your light cannot prove your name

let birds fly

there is duty is there freedom when working for the people

when you smile you also try to let the caged bird out to fly

the truth should be enough for who's mind cannot believe

that they have worked too hard to long

and the chains or cages are gone

there are rules is there reason

why work should be so hard

that one is never early

and for others its too late

we're driven mad before were thirty

or are knackered before forty

if we lead we push the pace

and the pace becomes a law

there are questions are there answers

to the problems we become

if we learn to lead ourselves or forget
what we have done

we age forget and learn in that we move
on

and freedom a bird that flys we should
not prey upon

lost myth

special times in life like secrets

are more precious as time marches on

the page that turns the story

away from the chapter where it begun

this means there is also myth

enough to destroy the weapon

enough to create belief

or a system we depend on

birthdays are for everyone

before we all forget

remember what is equal

to a beast it is a pet

at Christmas who we've lost

would be welcome to appear

if they say that they are Jesus

would they get hell out of there.

the falling stars

the colour of art and the blood in our
hearts

are together as wings that play in the air

turning toward soaring above and
silently landing

the books from our brains are that we
will maintain

the standard of life and prevent suffering

the songs we sing are are of what we
dream everything

and if we move as one time will stand
still

that we can see through the doubt

perhaps as we age we see through the
rage

and leave others another way out

that peace be upon us and not at a price

that love will recover the freedom of
flight

and angels will settle and rest their wings

that we will have hearts like the birds
that sing

The rising current

the fish aren't scared of the water

so what does it matter to me

treading where sharks are much fatter

who talk of the screams in the sea

the pride of the jungle will hunt

and remember where futures could be

while hyenas will laugh in arrogance

at their share is this how it be

the vultures could circle for ever

in deserts rising air

what does that mean to a spider

that waits patiently there

on the ocean floor there's also law

life without the language

and that's the way it is

once you've learned enough of the
language

because we see not in the dark

and how could fishes see a shark

when all that lights the sleeping sea

are things that could not be

the angel of the war

save yourselves or be at war it is the
human error

keep the truth in your heart speak about the terror

reaching out of the fire medicine is more

calm a creature of creation the angel of the war

can our words be worth hearing if our voice isn't one

can the music in our lives be silenced by a gun

when the sun goes down for who will it rise

when the weapons of war can ruin the skies

life is half of the battle especially for cattle

there are medals made of metal and coins worth more

we see the price of a life peeping out of a hole

take aim and fire death cannot be told

walk to work

keep your dream secret they fade if you share

because we are the people who challenge or dare

to say where we are going and only on foot

and what we would do if we put on a boot

the system would mean that you wake up alarmed

without enough time to sing like a bird

leaving your home you remember the key

but the key to your dreams is who you should be

stay on a side that is not a lie

and remember how many without you would cry

we die on our own unless we make errors

and don't get involved with the loss of the terrors

we leave love alive and hate will not matter

because fate has the time where people know better

than to fuel the wars or the people that cause

the absence in life or dreams to be shattered.

3. MINDS THAT ARE FREE

MINDS THAT ARE FREE have a colourful world

like ships in the sea or skies to a bird

minds that are free are not bound by fear

look in your heart for one that is near

to the world we'll achieve and time we'll steer

through wars too long and harvests bare

so the poor get fed instead of bombs going off

minds that are free believe in only enough

enough means necessary not more than any

and a piece of pie should only cost a penny

do the maths there's less bullets for guns

the cargo is bread the basket is tons

minds that are free are a means to an end

friends we can make and laws we can bend

like bridges that stretch over the sea

as high as you like and where god can see

minds that are free are able to learn

the path of time without reaching higher

and wisdom is there instead of magic

this way is the path out of the fire.

the dead tomorrow

the gun is loaded in our hands pointing to the temple

give me hands to pull it down the sickness it is mental

keep the saviors sailing round time we want to follow

know that weapon in our hands is a dead tomorrow

time is leaking to the tombs what life's essence is

why we die why we try and if we were alone

come from where your mind can't win
can't you smell the fear

blame the devil call it sin then it might
appear

the ship is coming to the shore powered
up with lightning

on board the reasons for the wars
weapons we've been selling

who is the captain of the ship that we
would all believe in

when what we're told is we're too old

to stop the war repeating

the crew are young the ship is new
locked and loaded

the times are spun the enemy a
generation not wanted

the balance of life separate from the rules
of war

the dead tomorrow is a day when war
becomes the law

silent hearts

silent hearts live in dark cages of this age

where are the keys that will exit this
stage

is it cheap or expensive to fly in the sky

can we still go to heaven after we die

the rythum of drums steers the night

love is the song and can do no wrong

the house it is happy with dancing and cheer

however the party is for who is not there(in memory of)

a bird it is roosting and knows it will roast

it pecked at the chips and it pecked at the toast

the way we are living just waiting for god (having given up)

explains too why mans best friend is a dog

we scream at the counter for only free range

but none can be heard because of the rage

that would allow hunting for nothing but sport

and the caging of birds without a thought

when your heart is silent waiting is long

and death is an angel to tell that it's wrong

to imprison a bird or take who is waiting

for life after death at this stage of the making

in our hands

keepers of hardened hearts suffer like the statues

stuck in traffic snuffing magic standing for it all

advancing years rule the budget and our nuclear fears

but in the arms of creation our world it has no cares

for what we've planted or who is haunted

or death dealing it's card

the land of the Bascavilles has a dog called Spot

because it was so big it was cornered and shot

but out of the story the law needs it's glory

and so mans best friend is a dog

in the dark summer evenings on the
green pastures

what would we ask of god

to guide and protect us in the middle of
nowhere

or to tell us where is the shop

keepers of the dark land buy nothing that
is second hand

and spirits lurk where folk need work
surely by laws

can we get by just as sinners needing
nothing more

than what we can hold in our hands love
peace or war

the drifting art

thorns of fire climb the sky claiming rain
of tears

roses red from blood that's shed reach the
present years

roots hold fast to handled hearts earth
within their grip

the desert yields empty space for flowers
are it's ship (flowers disappear into the
desert)

sailing through the arc of time days spin
into months

the waves of war are settling peace
becomes a chance

nations they are gathering all must now
account

upon their need for weaponry devils
leave in doubt

thorns of fire claim the sky climbing
clouds singled out

the wish for water drifting past and
vanishing

where are we that we must shout help the
people live

when all the efforts of the humans means
that we must give

chances to the people are a chance to the
world

if one man be the enemy let the rest be
heard

that food and water be the goal upon the
desert shores

that people do not chance the sea
avoiding holy wars

love between the people locks them into
land

and let the roses also grow upon the
desert sand

in our hands we have the message
beating in our hearts

that war and evil cannot win against the
creators art

for this world we hope

seek a fine isle surrounded by sand

its mountain a myth turned into a castle

inside it are dreams that jostle and bustle

find in it light from the start of the day

see through the illusions of hatred and
power

and where you can see one is there a fire

the echoes of time not seconds or
minutes

are waves that can wash this fire away

cement mixed with sand steals the land
in units

the corners of kingdoms and co ordinates
of lives

crystals of colour are counted as value

but coins in a box are not bees in a hive

flowers have sense to turn to the sun

who would we turn to before war begun

to spread like a virus infecting the peace

of who is responsible I've said the least

love is to conquer the system that kills

for all of it's money we still need wills

the battles are there people all matter

raising the money for bread and for butter

everyone is useful that keeps the peace

but nations will fight over prices to keep

their people in power and smoke in the sky

god help this world they are willing to die

4. KINGDOMS

days we would discover

the head of the wind a course on the sea

a ship that was lost returns to be free

from the earth colour rust and salt water

from the world where we lost to the order

pollen scented dreams come ashore

flowers commanded by wind after war

wheels are still round and gravity bound

the order a win that no one has found

the head of the wind peace from the past

no smoke drifting by the city
skyline

curves on the waves are light
from the sea

and the cirrus the height it
might actually be

the month named Armageddon
in years we cannot count

the future has it happened and is
it a way out

from the fear that stops our
hearts

on days we would discover

forgotten hopes

the feeling of forgotten hopes

is in their eyes

they sail around the island

searching for lost times

history a bullet in the gun

slavery a weapon that would kill
everyone

under the sea the answer to world war

but up on the island there's no people
anymore

under the sun the sky is blurred with
smoke

over the land the victory that no body
would want

chains from the past attached to the mast

the cannons are all silent from the means
of the blast

a day not in the papers that would come

decisions that were made for the world
population

the years they are now not guarded by
the guns

the end of all the hopes and deeds

thy kingdom come

the buzz

the echo in an empty room

cools the peaks of summer

water is a season

is there any for a stranger

the engines thirst for autumns air

screaming at their driver

exhausted ideas result in loss

and facing what we fear

in the sea the salt of us

there is life below its dust

even in the darkest depths

life can still protect itself

and with the echo of the engine

what the hell are we defending

sailing on fuel what has been dead
(organic fuel oil)

our hearts are cold our blood is red

even in the age of flight

humans had within their sight

that freedom flys and justice falls

where will we be when freedom calls

not washed in water sailing past

a parting wave that none live past

and why birds fly is not to meet us

on that last day the sea will greet us

well come to Africa

if there's love in the universe
how far would it be from here
if this world is a worthy ship
why would we be going there

while famine stamps upon the crops
our ballast tanks are full of rocks
and if we choose to weigh the anchor
the compass points to east of Africa

the flood and drought not a dreadnought
but the damage has been done
a symbol of this worlds love for war
of what would your ship become

out classed feared or remembered

for sinking bombing or raising hell

while injustice turns nations to deserts

and islands get flooded as well

then never be in ballast

unless it's water your bringing to shore

there is always a welcome in Africa

and there are wells we'll put in some
more

a tear in the ocean

a drop in the ocean what is it to you

standing on gravity or floating in the sea

the world is in motion and circles the sun

alone in the emptiness complete as one

a heavenly blue in the blackness of space

a tribute to life a statement of grace

a gift from our god and treasure for lesser

bound for eternity the earth locked in weather

the rain it will come so feel the first drops

and thirst for the measure that waters the crop

that all will be fed by the miracle potion

and blood it is red that it shouldn't be seen

a drop in the ocean what is it to you

that you are the one time belongs to

and even on the speeding world

your feet are steady and words they are
heard

the drops of the ocean are not in fact
tears

but they are of the same value and
amount to our fears

as souls in the universe we store them
somewhere

and sail into days that will become years
(we sail on fears)

famine of theft

until the end the wind will gather grains
of pollen

until the harvest comes to be all of it is
nothing

until the rain and sun are done the earth
will support life

but take away the gift of god if nothing
does arrive

the mountain of bread upon the sea

enough for you enough for me

grains of wheat upon the fleet

to fight against the famine

the floods and drought are causing doubt

farmers they would worry

when the gift of life they're losing

means that everyone is sorry

save those people from that end

let them know they have a friend

the world is bigger than the bounty

and a bowl holds much rice

are their leaders kings of men

that none could offer help to them

and kingdoms come to nothing

if its nothing they believe.

5. MOUNTAIN OF MYTH

dragon smoke

there's a mountain of myth with cliffs by the sea

inside the nests are hearts that fly

up on the wind to the top of the cliffs

and down to the sea to discover its myths

circles of coins are seen in the shallows

the eyes of the dragon watch upon each

for the touch of a body and sign of a soul

the land smells of lemon and feels like a peach

but who has lost their hearts has hope

and souls that roam need dragon smoke

to join the one's who are among the
angels

and to raise what life can be

into time the lock of all keys

the dragon will fly claiming night

but where dreams will arise seeds open

hope is the house on top of this mountain

dragon smoke and let me be free

I'm just a soul searching the sea

I never came to this land with a gun in
my hand

what I've seen I'll never say it is so

because it's a problem if everything goes
up in dragon smoke

dragon tears

as the dragon breaths fire into the water

birds fly over the ocean

the rain through the smoke a mythical
potion

of endless reach in opposite ways

that no one should go into such a corner

as where a dog would die

this pool of fuel fills cars at the pump

and planes rise into the air

we all would go on a summer holiday

but we cannot bring a fear

of leaving behind gravity

and feeling the flutter

like young birds leaving the nest

in trees above the gutter

the city's square lights and black corners

are places that life leads

and from there too its possible

to raise up like seeds

of life if water is there

and of fires if we cannot share (tea
instead of water)

the dragon breathes fire into the water

so humans float above the slaughter

the dolphins play at the bow of the ship

the propellor and steering a crown and
whip

the anchor of faith slips through the net

the cargo we keep is the size of a pet.

a freedom fort

my joy is her freedom what has its course

a beauty that challenges every voice

not heard in the battle or seen at war

not lost in the sea or able to fall

when once I was wicked i felt in my soul

an erring from where life was the goal

and freedom from that is the heart in us all

love is her child and peace be the call

freedom can see the effort of eyes

that strain upon age and read between
lines

the truth it is buried deep in our minds

and where would we be but behind
enemy lines

under the rainbow freedom must win

the red and the black upon brown upon
green

and only the colours of love will appear

when time it is done and death it is near

she smiles like the sunshine we welcome
each day

the strength in her heart is a place we can
stay

and without the walls that make up the
borders

freedom can win and can restore the
orders

bright

lunar light on the sea

tell a story to me

of the beauty she has

not the secret she keeps

silver blackness to spend

a coin to the end

we sail on our names

but make war with our brains

I will always be free

from chains left in the sea

that keep the people apart

in our eyes is our art

freedom can reach the sky

there is no one to buy

or to take away the life

from the people to be

she has given me joy

through the story I am

I'll do all that i can as a reasonable man

to keep the past where it is and the future
bright

no tears in our eyes because for freedom
we fight

ebony eyes yield apple pips

the darkest grave could sink our ships

with waves that wash the island bare

of who she is and why we care

knot of wood

a door its roots are holding it shut

the hell it is the fire its not

the flattened forests are locked away

the grandfather clocks are trying to say

demons are born after dealers in death

the rain came from heaven to wipe out
whats left

the cows have gone mad with fear of
their own

for the falling of bombs on the cities of
stone

then open the door with the chisel and
saw

look on the answers to nuclear war

out of the forests crushed on the day

the wind through the willows is war on
the way

death is an angel not leading the way

who had a choice was not willing to stay

with the war upon the seasons

god gave us life but who has the reasons
(good cause)

the door to summer

snow flakes melt until they shine seeds
undone wake

from the ground they twist and climb to
reach the open air

shapes and sizes white and dark in time
with natures spin

begin the dance of evergreen the season
is now spring

red and green make brown the robins
wings appear

on the brown of broken branches he sits
and sings to some

of the broken spell of winter it's rusty
clock undone

life returns to take it's place underneath
the sun

the mountain river icy diamonds of the
sun

sparkle with the starlight beauty from
before

can we find the door to summer does it
lead to war

do we have a day a year or season to
explore

the love that is you

knowing only love that's true
I have a wish I wish for two
of hearts that fly into the night
that stirs our dreams into a sight

having our dreams to believe
I see in them that we conceive

the waking day where our love rules

the stars are set and are our tools

we will meet just for love

see we have that power

it takes many to keep us apart

but of love do they have any (no)

knowing only love that's due

the hearts that fly belong to you

that are not caged or kept in sight

the dream it is of freedom flight

when the birds come back

nests of time lined with black silk

built in the corners of kingdom come

the wings on the city instead of the
smoke

hopes for the future freedom to come

the flocks they are fledging

and lightning does crack

the shells they are falling

from hell we come back

the stone come to life

and heaven is rising

the call in the air

without advertising

the pigeon polite to us on our way

the colours of Christmas black white gray

souls also fly between the cities

survivors sail the sea

who asks for love

the love that is you consumed me like
fire

out of this world my heart flying higher

than stars left alone in the coldness of
space

the light in our eyes signals the truth

I see through the black also the white

to where we might be at the end of that
flight

a beautiful world surviving the last

with looks from the future at souls from
the past

ghosts they are gathered with nowhere to
go

they pick on their food they reap and
they sow

left in this world they are not without
you

your love for me is why I'm about you

for them there is prayers for us there is
song

for safety in their numbers but for us
there is one

to believe is a task not given to many

and who asks for love does not have any

6. SHE IS NO ILLUSION

a friend of freedom

she is no illusion
beauty belong
I write for her poems
and sing for her songs

that freedom is in her
and not secret or dark
that she can see hope
in whats there of my art

why people bother

to fully undress

is to be clean

not to bow their heads

from sadness guilt

or other losses

freedom finds

its friends.

a night to win

how the smile in your eyes

tears the stars from the skies

and the colour of your hair

is the dark that's still there

when we walk through the night

with the moon shining bright

I see there's no compare

to the love in the air

for the coming of the day

we will stand and not pray

and our dreams of above

will be proved like our love

when we turn to the truth

there's a way we can answer

the hopes that we have

for a world that will win

c.

a night to win for everyone

a nature to begin

a light to shine behind the dark

to enter to win

away with war

do we wake up in heaven

are we sleeping through hell

is there no one amongst you

that can ring the bell

that will wake who is needed

or locate the door

where people can go to

to finish the war

are we standing on earth

or flying above

to get to the people

who believe in love

if we sit for a moment

or need to lie down

who carries the light

that we will be found

not wanting for war

or dealing in death

not lacking a life

and only ourselves

can come through the paths

that made us this way

that peace has a chance

and that war goes away

I choose her

the tide climbs the rocky shores

away from the deep and the dark

the sun shines revealing the laws

that evaded the schools of the shark

the beautiful beach bends with nature

no telling the age of the line

and her footprints upon it

are leading the way from the end and beginning of time.

she sees the horizon and size of the sun

she endangers the enemy with rocks not a weapon

their ships will sink and there planes will crash

blood out of a stone just like bangers and mash

her beauty is seen and not something to hide

if your heart turns to stone discover her side

that there is no horror worth laughing about

and that mother nature will have the last shout

the beauty of ages

the moments of millennia

hinge about our words

that true is true

and up to you

to discover

freedom flys ahead of swords cut
through with rust

mountains rise above valleys

again ploughed into plains

deserts grow life strains

the seconds of the season

are challenges to life

the world will have a reason

for putting up with life

but beauty softens hatred

that has ruined much of nature

and it just so happens

humans have perfected such a creature

the every ones England

if everyone had a crown in England

what would they have to buy

if everyone had to live in England

there would be no space to die

with the war so close natures a ghost

the people are left requiring a host
someone to believe in

we built too much to have and dug
beyond life's levels

finding light that could not be
discovering the devil

medicines when not prescribed could
make you see the same

and the drug that we're used to is not to play the devils game

open fire.

the roots of time are under foot

armies were conquered

the nests of birds that are not cooked

stacked upon the cliffs

road signs and street art

features on the journey

out of the castle

we have built out of our money

we arrive on time at the shore of the land

waiting for the ship to issue a command

the ship is a secret that all have to keep

but where it is going is not for the sheep

the sea it boils into their cups

raises its decks and has an army of mops

that fly into heaven with wizards on top

the noises it makes are so war will stop

leave it says leave leave with ghostly echos

but a story like this no one would believe

that logic is magic when seen from the past

and magic will do if the ship takes a blast.

7. THE DEATH OF ROSES

black roses

the death of roses in a jar

brings the bees from where they are

to sit upon a velvet throne

and claim the essence for their own

nothing tells them where we are

but stars that shine are near not far

what is lost upon the way

can lead the rest from yesterday

so leaders left in history books

are only there to those who look

and if you've learned from one of them

learn the book then use the pen

to challenge hatreds ugly war

save the roses from the jar

the scent of summer the setting sun

love and hope our work is done

so all would have time to rest

where war was once let me suggest

that peace can be within our reach

where flowers grow and teachers teach

where the school has been burned down

tell the world of that poor town

where hatred costed even more

than who was forced to join the war

but to share

summer says so very well

what people know but do not tell

that love will gather in the air

as if a spirit standing there

all i have is but to share

and angels will remove my fear

of what this world will become

for who survives the wars that come

there is no clue to who has offended

only to people who have pretended

that they care enough to stand

where god would put his hand

in this world we can be sure

that all are equal in gods law

and that the borders that are built

are from the peoples blood that spilled

upon the fields and on the hills

voices claim the sky

because in this world we do not kill

in peace we only die

GIVE YOUR LIGHT

a fading star bursts into light supernova stellar night

command the ship that's in your hand

below the stars a sea of sand

as the seasons slip from our world the deserts grow

the world sealed like an hour glass

so raise a harvest in your heart

what puts the nations off the chart

feel the course of blood within

and tell your brain your heart can win

the battle set upon this world against the litter bug

a mass of litter that came to life from the wars nuclear waste

a ship that built itself

the litter bug that frightens off the little bird

with it's echoing of time

the little birds wings ring with more echos of time

into a fine tuned harmonic vibration

inside we feel it as love

give your light to god above

lights lead the ships but the ship of death
is amongst them

a fading star bursts into light

keep your borders out of sight

people are not so stuck in graves

and slaves are free upon the waves

make your home how it should be

then set the other people free

from what they think you are inside

with truth there is nothing to hide(clean
seas)ed9 c f

circles of vultures

taste my air in whats left of our ways

smoke before the ending of winter

I'll save the world i swear on your graves

but humans will follows the circles of
vultures

the tap has been tapped the sea level
rising

the food it is stacked the price is
surprising

the kilo of meat so easy to choose

is of the same beast so easy to loose

death it is dealing in more than the dollar

some humans in furs and dogs pull at
their collar

to bring down the beast that went to fetch
weather

some birds are gone for ever and ever

it is the wind that is howling and out of its jaws

the waves that are reaping the coast and our shores

the island is flooded systems shut down

the hills are the islands where people are found

alone with their language an ignorant bliss

the last generation how fitting it is

that all doing nothing was forever enough

to damn the machine so the killing would stop

an explosion of lies

steel stands where buildings were

bent buckled from the bomb

the church open the steeple gone

tower blocks with corners torn

to the wind a dune is born

rectangular voids filled in time

random bunches of plants grow

between the pavings and broken window

silent skies scan for lives

that somehow would survive the bomb

the lies that launched it

could have stretched into an everlasting
one.

8. THE LAND OF DREAMS

if the truth dies

the land of dreams escapes all reason

human laughter finds its end

not enough to feed the people

of the price who can pretend

they have not met grim the reaper

set upon the common kind

who are not sat down with the preacher

preaching stories to the blind

the land of lies is always sleeping

never waking to the truth

medication that they're taking

makes them old and put to proof

we are not the total in

the world we've turned into a bin

and because we're taking out

the managers will curse and shout

that the land of life is for the living

all have been proved to be dead

in what futures will be coming

to human kind the word was said

science is something to believe

the weather tells us more

than science ever could do

even as the law

love and hate

love evolves in our minds and becomes
the light

we see through the pain so then we
would fight

for freedom that flys not justice that falls

upon people that live under the law

a look in the eyes tells us if we're in love

from the earth we are bound to the stars
up above

and the circles of black are just as the
void

what crushes the stars what ships do
avoid

but we steal a smile that would steer us
away

from the paths we would take and truth
we would say

that would bring down the hate to its
original devil

when life is challenged hatred is level

we focus we think on what we can learn

while dreams will float on the heaviness
of hate

and sleep is silent into the night

that ship we know steers to our fate

nature cures

as sure as the sun will rise

our planet we are warming

we know the sun will grow

but its not us that its harming

nature cures and nurtures

it tells us what we've done

it shows us what results have been

and the way that will become

wars will have to wait

and angels will be asking

why people dealt in fate

and without who we will be working

hunger should be what drives

the engine in the car

in mirrors we should see the knowledge
that we are

destined for results upon a world of
matter

and surely to experience what is left of
honor.

love mountain

shes there when i need her

like the winters rising sun

we share in the solutions

the problems do come

for us we are in love

so wars will not matter

wars will end with moments

while love lasts forever

can mountains fall from where they stand

and there do angels gather

we walk beside them foot on land

for us we face the weather

so what is it that eagles dare

they prey upon the feather

and who digs up the mountain looking
for the treasure

the bird in the storm

silent clouds are summoned
to the circle in the air
the storm has eyes that fly
humans have no fear

freedom has its wings
where would it appear
we guard the bird that sings
eagles need not dare

from out the cage we come
tumble weeds that run

not separate from our path

upon the iron world

lightning cracks thunder rolls

the page in heaven turns

we read the stars and find the sun

without corners to world

we are the bird in hand

its nest built in the bush

in a defending pyracantha

with berries it can crush

the sun sines within us

the night was swept into a wedge of
black

the sun was held in a basket

the heavens were seen to be worlds about
stars

and the hills and the valleys were rid of
the cars

the wedge was knocked into the foot of
the mountain

instead of the church they all went to the
fountain

the sun that is in us started to shine

the world without winter is nearly the
time

the days are now with us that where we must go

we must lead as the light though there isn't a show

and remember the winter was times we were fed

and the sun now shines as a basket of bread

give out the loaves that would bring them together

bury a chain to anchor the weather

tell them a word that they would believe

a name not a gun that they would have to retrieve

accretion disc

music searches through the black

spheres of fire sing

the edge of time is dancing

and the song is how to win

the quiet peace between the stars

and the love of Venus next to mars

come and hear it with me now

and be among the people

I'll play the song we love so much

until the stars twinkle

another day in greater circles

spinning past the sun

let us reach into the temple

of deeds that we have done

the earth will always hold the moon

closer than the stars

and that night has come to us

the world is truly ours

hold on to a dream

of bubbles in the air

and see the beauty of it all

our life is that we share

why birds fly

when honesty is what you see fight
against the lies

when what you say will pay the day look
into their eyes

to have enough means we can share

but greedy people like to stare

then make no effort of the show

our minds are also hungry

feed your body and your mind

your soul will know such hunger

find the best thing in your mind for a
boxer it is anger

feel enough to know who's hurt and why
they would wander

but try to be most alert to who you would
require

as friend or family in these times

between these types there are not much crimes

when honesty is whats required stand upon the truth

if all around you falls below it wasn't made of proof

what we say can raise the day and also make birds fly away

but silence is as violence to a soul that needs to know

and birds will leave an island that they do not want to know

the bright horizon

if ever i should meet you

would you notice something new

between the colours of sky and of the
world were coming to

could you stop or try to find out if our
lives were really won

and that the history that repeats itself

are the days that never come

we're years apart between the hunger

and what mankind would rather do

would you listen to the voices

that with hell would come through

the days of war and months of famine

that the people still endure

can we count the days of plenty

with our ships tied to the shore

we're on the bright horizon

where else would our world now be

and like a clock we face the world that
will always try and see

the examples that are made when
progress brings in more

and the day when the cause of hunger is
also against the law

9. WITHIN OUR DREAMS

I've travelled in time and found myself old

but the world it is hurting from people so bold

so i offer my plate to who would come here

and wait for the one to whom I'm so near

then I'll love without hurt for the rest of my days

because play without love should be beyond the grave

I feel in the morning the strength to go
on

living below the threat of the nuclear
weapon

I need in the evening to chew with my
jaws

so let none of my enemies enter my
doors

because love is not mercy and will
always defend

these words are my wealth I am rich to
the end

Freed animals

the last of the primitives of nuclear fear

aimed at the world as if it wasn't there

raising the enemy who have never had
fun

giving them excuses like the use of a gun

the last of the species wiped off the list

the third to reach space that's how crazy
it is

the vet says the pigs would love to eat truffles

but what would they do with the rifles

a foot on the world or a shovel below

why we would stand and where we would go

if decisions are made for all of us now

how many alive how many now

I remember when the light shined in your hair

and all the world was left behind and no one else was there.

we steer in our world

our world reaches out holds the moon

with magnetic lines bulging into space

meteors pass through to nothing

or gravity brings them down

comets burn their way to oblivion

and asteroids collide in their fields

planets are spun round their stars

galaxies spiral and spread

our sphere is solid apples are lush

segments of orange contain love

in lines like flux or piff and peel

with one in your hand its hard to steal

the nebula or cosmic drift creating stars

the circle of blackness is their absence
consuming them

into the incredible night eternity

and star light a sphere of warmth

reaches toward infinity

the universe is without limits direction
gets nowhere

what crosses our paths is that we only
steer

to the completion of work in an
everlasting sum

like the seed of a crystal and a corner
stone

that's in your heart or in your home

battery hen

the sign says do not walk on the water

the traffic lights say stop

the boat to the ship is in working order

the planes still taking off

the light house beams above the rocks

and thin ice breaks below the clocks

the sign says I'm not on the water

and the innocent go running off

they play with nature in the yard

and notice weeds near to the fence

they have sweets to eat and seeds to plant

the world will make sense

can their efforts like the shells of seeds

be as easily undone

and if they are what are we to say

of the world it will become

some how the sun still shines

on crystal waters near the shores

take some steps on to the land of laws we
can endure

and find the key to mercy under the cat
where we left it

for quicker meals the battery hen is a
bird that is protected

so why not go to where the species is more free

far away on a farm or somewhere by the sea

the broken cage has come of age

for birds let it be

I believe that I've found it

moon beams over silver sea bring a star back to me

that fell into a crystal fountain high upon a golden mountain

where tears fly and birds prey where spirits go but do not pay

the size of it we keep in jars in the future it will power cars

wait with me near the shining stream

but if you find it guard your dreams

that we'll return to look upon it

I believe that I have found it

close in loves eternal stare

beside the shores of mortal fear

opposite the tears that choke

some feel the sun some see the smoke

I believe that I've found it

that we can ride above the waves

or cut through bars that kept us slaves

or even steer the world we're on

through world war two and world war
one

so i believe I've found it

what wakes the birds before the day

what makes the enemy go away

the dream of falling through the air

and waking with a need to care

the love theme

there are the seasons and sky upon the world

there are flags and plastic bags for boys and girls

but in the night there is a sight

that puts us near to where the people have to fight(fear)

we're on a world without the power of a child

we breathe it's air that tastes like dust and also ice

and in between the leaves are green the gold is given

what would nature sacrifice

the moon is high so why should I fear

the coming wars like yesteryears

the tide is rising on the sand of our time

the sun is shining I believe that it is mine

I'll share with you in all we do we

will not die from what this world is coming to

the roves and houses stretched across the plain and hills

the ocean drops and waves that wash the worldly spill

within our dreams we are in teams

and out of the darkness of our eyes we see a beast

the morning comes with salt in the air

the dream is over so is the fear

but what we know is it could grow into the truth

and blow the walls out the house before the roof

we would not know it if we go but for those that did

we keep the peace that we should know.

The End.